IN THE DAYS OF CAGES

IN THE DAYS OF CAGES

POEMS

APARNA LANJEWAR BOSE

Foreword by Namdev Dhasal

Introduction by Sutinder Singh Noor

MANOHAR
2010

First published 2010

ISBN 978-81-7304-848-7

Published by
Ajay Kumar Jain *for*
Manohar Publishers & Distributors
4753/23 Ansari Road, Daryaganj
New Delhi 110 002

Typeset by
Ajay Arts
Delhi 110 002

Printed by
Salasar Imaging Systems
Delhi 110 035

Time tells me what I am
I change and I am the same
I empty myself of my life
And my life remains

—Mark Strand
(The Remains)

For my grandmother for all the grand times' sake
For teaching me to be different in a world of differences

Contents

Foreword

Poetry is an extremely powerful and superior genre in literary studies. It is the ubiquitous presentation, standing tall at the utmost summit of emotions, and something which one loves to hear again and again. It is fundamentally, so expressive that to understand it or to make it understandable, an uncalled for formality of words or appreciation is not required.

For those poets, desirous to fill their candidature in the poetic arena it's really something precious, giving them unbound pleasure.

My niece Aparna had asked me to pen a few words for her new collection *In the Days of Cages* and I was slightly rattled. I am of the opinion that a poetry collection should not have a foreword or should not have words at all; except of course the poet's poetry. But by telling her this I was not even ready to lessen her enthusiasm And therefore, out of my understanding and belief in her creation and for her love, I am attempting to write a few words, regarding her poetry, which I am sure, would be acceptable to all.

The history of Marathi literature is more than 700 years old. In this 700 to 750-year old glorious tradition with an exception to 3 or 4 literary creations and attempts of the Mahanubhavs, there's really nothing to lay down one's life for. My some time friend Drudhacharya Ashok Shahane, in the decades close to the 1960s had written an article on Marathi literature titled 'Ksh kiran' (Ksh kiran-X-Ray) and by doing so he had thereby fought the established Marathi literary tradition. After carefully screening it, he openly declared, how trash it was as literature.

The true literary movement in Marathi in genuine sense began in the 1960s with the little magazine movement. It challenged the literary cultural monopoly and proprietorship of the so-called elite-literary monopolizers' and authoritarians, by defeating and denying its literary aesthetical values. The activists of this movement discarded the literary aesthetical parameters of the established authoritarians, rejected the syntax, grammar and metre of poetry and enlivened poetry by giving her the ambrosia of blank verse.

If one were to exclude, *The Lidacharitra* (biographical narratives) of Mahanubhavs, the *Viranya* (intensely devotional songs metaphorically suggesting separation of the beloved from lover) of Gyaneshwar, the *Abhangas* (devotional poetry) of Saint Tukaram, Janabai and Chokhamela, the *Smritichitre* (memoirs) of Laksmi Bai Tilak, the poetry of Bahinabai Chaudhari, then what's left in this 700-year old history of Marathi? Simply nothing. Only stones.

In fact, the new stature, literary parameters and renewed vision that Marathi literature is accorded today was because of the little magazine movement.

This movement, consequentially, disrupted the suffocating and stifling atmosphere in Marathi literature by paving a new and untrodden path. And only to later carve a majestic path out of it, the other most important literary movement, besides the little magazine movement, that became a pervasive and forceful literary presentation of the lives of the masses, was the Dalit literary movement.

Truly speaking, the Dalit literary movement was heralded, even before the little magazine movement, by Mahatma Jyotiba Phule. And even prior to Phule, it was Chokhamela, who challenged the proprietary rights and monopolization of the haute monde and the elect-literary authoritarians. And therefore, in modern Marathi literature his reference can be considered as a literary touchstone so to say. Not only Marathi literature, but the entire corpus of Indian literature that was mercilessly butchered by the controversy over noble Sanskrit lineage, was freed to a great extent by the little magazine movement, Dalit sahitya movement, and the cultural and literary movements of the Left political parties.

In fact, we are well aware that in literary arts, along with each generation, new literary paraphernalia builds up. The controversy over superiority claims and fine aesthetics within Sanskrit sahitya had made a stagnant pool of the complete body of Indian literature. The stagnant waters of this pool were released, and their hindrances were broken by the already mentioned movements. And my generation of litterateurs has got the rightful legacy and heritage of all these movements.

Aparna's mother Jyoti *Tayi* (*Tayi*—affectionately means elder sister) Lanjewar is a prominent name in Marathi literature as also in Dalit sahitya, as being part of a potent Phule-Ambedkar literary tradition movement. Her foremost, all-pervasive presence in Marathi literature is that of a talented poet, and activist. Not that Aparna has chosen to tread the same path of poetry, but that this path was also essential and inevitable for her. And this fact cannot be refuted.

In contemporary Indian literature there are many big names—spreading arts and literature in the English language. Their creativity has been so terribly affected by self and personal awareness that it has become perverted and virtually fallen into oblivion, as regards to the collective pain and pathos of others.

Especially, the Indian writers writing in English dealing with limited problems in their writings, are in fact, dealing with the problems pertaining to just a handful of elitist—the *beau monde*—high society groups. Neither, are these writers conscious about social transformation nor do they find it necessary to depict the pain and suffering of the oppressed marginalized Dalits.

Our outworn culture which is more than 500 years old has invariably been stigmatized by such handful of so-called literary monopolizers and proprietors. And this is not a closely guarded secret any more. This very culture of no clarity and transparency, that had kept the Dalit-Bahujans/ former untouchables away from proprietary rights, power, education and a dignified living, was for the first time, gun powdered and blown, by Phule-Ambedkar in true sense. And because of this, all the creative paths finally opened up before the Dalits here.

The little magazine movement and Dalit literary movement by their very contemporary and original literary sensibilities, have contributed immensely to Indian literature. They provided it a post-modern opportunity and approach because of which contemporary Indian literature is seen greatly enriched by new sensibilities, consciousness, new ideals and symbols. It thus, became consciously receptive to universality.

Aparna's poetry is a remarkable manifestation of a talented artist. Her poetry consciously illuminates her creative prowess and is a conscientious reminder of the spirit and self-respect of the marginalized. Till late, in our country poetry was considered as a genre dealing with extreme personal awareness or personal ignorance and one can say that the so-called big names here who write in English are good masters of it. Aparna's poetry is however, quite exceptional. Her poetry in this collection is a direct heir to the new artistic creativity, aesthetic value and style. Even in her most intensely personal poems, I hear the collective weeping voices of countless many. In the ebb and fall of the oceanic roars—the collective cries and in the white flurry of the waves—the endorsement of the collective pathos.

As a poet Aparna is known to me right from her school-going age. I distinctly remember some 20 to 25 years back when I was chairing the Asmitadarsh Sahitya Sammelan that was taking place at Nagpur—the second capital of Maharashtra and also an important base of Ambedkar's movement. After my speech, in between during the interval,

Jyoti *tayi* invited me home and treated me to a sumptuous meal. After the lovely lunch, Jyoti *tayi*, her husband and similarly my other literary friends and activists, we all started chatting and discussing things. At that moment a cute little, girl with a huge school bag, on her juvenile shoulders, entered calling 'Aai aai' Jyoti *tayi* who called her close and said 'Look who is here Dhasal mama . . . he is a poet . . . etc.' By telling her thus Jyoti *tayi* made the connection of how Aparna in her little age composes poetry.

After listening to this, I asked Aparna to read some of her poems. She was barely 8 or 9 then. She was a little shy but very soon overcame it all and got the stimulation when her father and I pressed her to read her poems. Finally, she did read, not one, but 3-4 poems she had composed in English. I was completely astounded, almost speechless for a while. At her young age, on seeing her remarkable, rather incredible understanding, and poetic sensibility, I was totally bowled nay surprised by her. And at that moment I felt like this little girl will carve a name for herself in the literary world and yes this is exactly what has happened.

Today, seeing her collection in print, the greatest joy and happiness is mine. I can feel in her poetry, the pain and suffering of the oppressed-margins, the joys and celebrations of womanhood; cry and anguish of loneliness; existential concerns; revulsion and revolt against hypocrisis of the world she is surrounded by, and her poetic protestation to the same. These all become pertinent through her poetry which can be felt by others as well. Her abandonment of fine aesthetics of the elites becomes evident in her 'In Response to What a Known Poet Said to an Unknown' while poems like 'When I Announced Today' spell her final verdict.

However, what also becomes obvious to all is Aparna's poetry and her poetic style, its poetic manifestation and presentation, is quite unlike these so-called literary elites and 'proprietors'. And this is what makes her poetry unique and different.

I am truly confident about her poetry.

To Aparna for her poetic oeuvre and future literary endeavours I give my good wishes and blessings.

Aparna go ahead!

Mumbai, 2009 NAMDEV DHASAL*

* The writer needs no introduction. Founder of the Dalit Panther in 1972, a militant organization modelled on the Black Panther in the US. In 1999 he received the most covetous Padmashree award given by the Government of India. In 2004 India's national academy of letters, Sahitya Akademi honoured him with, the only Lifetime Achievement Award it gave during its golden jubilee celebrations. He remains one of the greatest poets in India today.

Introduction: The Structurality of *In the Days of Cages*

> *The literary theorist killed poetry—dead because with their shrivelled hearts and swollen brains they are incapable of spotting a metaphor, let alone a tender feeling, is one of the more obtuse critical platitudes of our time. . . .*

Terry Eagleton is grappling with this problematic in his 'How to Read a Poem', and I have seen some other critics also facing this problem. It means the poetic genre is in crisis. Whenever I read a new poet I am always in search of poetry, poetic language, thematically poetic and how the poet is structurally conscious.

I have read the poems of Aparna Lanjewar Bose in *In the Days of Cages* and these poems have rebuilt my faith that those literary theorists should not lose confidence in this genre. Our new poets are well aware about the structural complexities of this genre. They know the futuristic signification of poetic language. They create not only the metaphor; rather they are capable enough to create the poetic signifiers. *In the Days of Cages* is that kind of signifier and Aparna's other language and signifiers are well defined through Cage. Thematically this signifier is realistic as well as beyond this kind of semantics. This grammatology makes the creation poetic. She says 'Rhyme—rhythm—figures—imagery—intact'. She becomes 'poetic in un-poetic times'.

The consciousness of 'unpoetic times' and to become poetic is the beauty of her poetry. She is not conscious only about this problematic, she is well aware of what is happening in the literary/philosophic/epistemological world and how to create a dialogue with this kind of paradigm. She writes about Derrida's 'Deconstructions':

> It takes the maturity of
> An experience to perceive
> That little bit of reality
> Which is there and still not there
> To learn real from unreal
> And unlearn the learnt

The poetic genre is the most autobiographical genre, but not like the fictional genre. It creates a different language, aesthetically different with a foreground and with a selection and precision. The poet creates space and symbols, but conscious about the communication. Aparna knows these poetic nuances. She creates tensions, oppositions and binaries, and her poem becomes more expressive. 'The roof has become the floor', 'yet life lingers for a living housed in lifelessness', 'here in my room light has no colour', 'bleak light flickers', 'the room has no lock, yet unlocks only when others are locked', 'nothing is included here, yet nothing is excluded', this kind of tension in language, without creating a metaphor is the beauty of Aparna's poetry.

Poetry speaks through words and words are signs, but this process starts from 'silence'. It makes the unconscious of poetry. When I read this genre I always try to understand this 'unconscious'. I have tried to grasp the 'immeasurable silences' of Aparna's poetry:

> I float on the surfaces of these immeasurable silences
> A voice amidst voiceless-ness

She creates the binary of voice/voicelessness or 'silence', but she is conscious how to reach the 'word', what the 'chaos of words' is and how 'words need words' in this poetic activity. These words remind us about the concept of silence and word in Saussure, Barthes, Derrida, Bhartrihari, Nagarjuna and the poets who talk about the significance of 'word' in creative activity:

> Why do words need words
> To shield themselves
> From the chaos
> Created by words
>
> Why do words spell
> Confusion of words
> And then sit
> To vindicate
> By more confusion
> of words.
>
> And its still
> Only words
> That we have between us.

And in Aparna's poetry these 'words' are very powerful, thematically conscious about the reality. She is also conscious how T.S. Eliot and other poets understood this reality, how Eliot created the 'symbol' of 'wasteland', but Aparna's words do not depict only the reality, they satirize and make us conscious of what is missing, what we lack and why this 'wasteland' exists:

> In this wasteland
> Of the dead and impotents
> No polestar shines
> Nor music one hears by the ocean light
> No caresses come from the winds
> Nor lull from the springs
> No beauty lingers anymore on lips
> Nor strength prevails in fists

This is how Aparna's poetic word awakens in a paradigmatic journey.

Thematically, Aparna Lanjewar Bose's poetry covers a wide expanse. She has travelled the corners of the globe and her experience of the plurality of cultures is very wide. That is the reason; she speaks ideologically and with a conscious voice. She means what she says. She is very confident in her poetic discourse.

I believe in this poetry futuristically.

SUTINDER SINGH NOOR*

Vice-President
Sahitya Akademi

* The writer is India's leading literary theorist, writer, critic and also a celebrated name in Punjabi literature. He heads India's National Academy of letters, Sahitya Akademi as the Vice-President.

To Where I Belong

My existence was beginning to cause me some concern
Was I a mere figment of the imagination?

—Sartre

How I wish to pour like the sea
Battered by storms
And drink to hearts content
The tidal waves one after the other
But I cannot roar like the sea
Nor blow the zephyr hard
I cannot tame a single wave to fulfilment
Encircling in the eddies
A captured object
Tossed by the currents
I remain to where I belong

D. Suryawanshi

A Truth (This is for Real)

They think that they
Have the right
  to write about me
  to speak about me
  to look at me
  to name me

They will probably write

  A 'natural' romantic story
  Of a girl full of 'concessions'
    whose enslaved forefathers slogged door to door
    who was fed with sun, water, air and earth
    whose parents forsook her in the land of strangers

And they will write

  How her living was laden
  With troubles and sorrows
  How loneliness nibbled her thought
  And how time inflicted scars

They will speak

  A 'natural' truth in their native voice
  How father immersed in a 10 to 6 shift
  And how he got boozed on his way home
  How the furrows on mothers' hands widened
  And how she aged before her ageing
  How in their routine squabbles
  The kids agitated
  Shrieked—shivered in restless motion
  And how together they spent difficult days

And they will speak

Of him as messiah
Every one who'd seek my shelter
And in the name of a tolerant culture
With hatred they will spare
'Two select days' of the year
And then taunt my entire tribe
With erratic economics
As beneficiaries of government's unrestricted pity

They will watch

Holding hand-grenades
My going and coming hence
While blood-shooting eyes will rain
Vesuvius fireballs
Their caltrop gaze will then shower
Innumerable 'calling of names'
And their obsolete ancient look
Would scrutinize my attire

And they will watch

With 'programmed' pride
The imagined real
Now their analysis would decide
My tomorrow for me.

But they will never know

With what great tenderness
Grace was bestowed by my forefathers
With what doting love and sacrifice
My folks grew me up
How father taught courage to fight challenges
And how mother taught to accept them.

But they will never know

The joy of living in the philosophy
Of Revolt and Revolution

And the art of being 'cultured'
In their innate boast of 'their culture'

But they will never know

That the moment I stand
Their meetings get dissolved
And when I am not involved
A new rebellion is born to strike back at them

But they will never know

Life has been so beautiful
And I have no complaints.

Of Being

Rituals I find boring
Ill construed time wasters
Strewn over outdated scripts
Else
We are not less complex
In our horrific secular indulgence
Of 'The be all—know all' kind
In the delight of teaching words
Those were untaught.

Customs are such logs
Unmoved with time
Presumptuous preoccupations
Of unromantic minds
Enlivened with maddening roar
'Do this don't do that'

The 'ritual' of being a single woman
Daring to double-dare in a 'customized' world
Is what interests me.

My Pa Once Said to Me

My Pa once said to me
'No need to be sensitive
Sensitivity is killing'
(Yet he loved my momma so well)
So like a dutiful daughter
I decided to kill my soul
(No not Faustus like)
I internalized my Pa's image of me
'Rock against the wind'
I strove to become what he wanted me to be
Lived his Dream
'Conquer the un-conquered.'
Each time I sit to think
I think of what Pa thinks
Would he like it this way or that or thus

Living in a world of complexes
Beaten fishes—stormy clothes—pulp fiction
I am glad my sensitivity holds sense
Enough to write about him.

D. Surya.

In This Wasteland

In this wasteland
Of the dead and impotents
No polestar shines
Nor music one hears by the ocean light
No caresses come from the winds
Nor lull from the springs
No beauty lingers anymore on lips
Nor strength prevails in fists

Young brains rot
Old wait for the cycle to complete
In this garden—intellectual sterility
Like weeds has outgrown trees
Those do not afford a shaded recess
To the exhausted body.

They are selling the dreams
Of this dreamland to the needy.
Yesterday the 'canary was in full bloom'
A full stringed guitar—now one stringed
Tomorrow will be smashed on the branch

In this wasteland
Birds are blissfully unaware
What the future holds
A monstrous dawn awaits all.

I Simply Do Not Know

How does one name the nameless insecurities?
All seems well and moving
Still looms the fear—worries
Of known possibilities
If only living could be depicted
As a graphic Warli* art
To get an overview
It's that simple.

Thread by thread weaves the tapestry
How long and for what continues this endless strife
What a price to pay to reach
The known hollowness within
Fighting desires that have acquired a form
Who says it's all so simple
Is there any promise left?
I simply do not know

*Warli—paintings and sketches depicting the life and culture of the Warli tribes of Maharashtra.

If Only

I can feel my intestines squabble within
The nausea of seeing it again
The mirrored fragments—pipe dreams
Phantasmagoric togetherness
Option less routes
Pre to post fellowship.
Oh for drunken blindness
Or squalid deafness
Some cerebral amnesia
To rid enlightenment.

It's not for reality perceived
But the appearance
That diminishes joy
Discoverer's doom
Conformism strikes terror
Hard for the young physique
To deduce theories
'Of being and not being'
Or to hold
Beyond comprehension
A rationalist ideal

If only one was the night
Of significant sounds
Nestling behind the trees
Scaring away the demons
Of dark

D. SURYAWANSHI

Growing up

I wondered what it meant to grow up
I saw myself around meaninglessness
Of things apparently—eventually turning so
Often I wished then
If fate perchance may chance
To make me mean something
Loitering in my campus days
Organizing activities with others my age
I found me engrossed in enrapturing talks
Of things that never mattered much
As years passed by
I ascertained the nugacious side of me.

Then came the days
When I waged a 'bread battle'
But I learnt
I couldn't be what I could not anymore
That I could be what I should
That I could possibly do so
Not by withdrawing into
Pseudo intellectual debates
Of moron leaders-puppet nations
And their absurd policies
Or of bourgeois pretensions of obscure realities
Nor of indulgence in derisive flirtations
And mind boggling emotional games.

But
By seeing sense in reason
By facing the real me
I understood
What it meant to grow up.

The metamorphosis took place
I extended my creation
Into my vocation found satiation
Spoke on
Secularism, communalism, totalitarianism
On all possible 'isms' conceived.
I harboured faith that ultimately
Intellectuals—like minded folks
Would unite—join
Will support non-violent battles

Then
I see Godhra in saffron fiery eyes
Bombay in recurrent black nightmares
Marathwada in a cattle's diaphonic bellow
Graham Stein's widow sick
Of fortitudinal composure.

And
I sit in my home
Watching one of those favourite channels,
Waiting for groceries to be delivered,
Cheques to be signed,
Car oil to be changed,
Premium to be paid,
Careful of how I look,
How I talk.
Sipping another glass,
Of distasteful wine
Instead of being the real person
Who ought to strike back
And get ready—to shoot at sight.

Spinsterhood

Hiding my spinster'd bruises under
Surveillance of 'husbanded' wives
'Kidded' mothers
Preaching me strong wedded vows
And the necessity of motherhood
Telling me the time of the day

I wondered who they reassured
Was it remorse of what was lost?
Or then
Of what could not be recovered

I wish I could tell them
Aren't we all pink within and within the pink?

And I still feel so deeply human inside.

Go On

I leave with lasting impressions
Of someone
Some moment.
Vague memories
Dine with the day
Cast my countless aspersions
On the need to be 'lasting'
Of occupying the high pedestal
Of know not what
Glory may be

Wrecking vengeance on the strength
Pushing pillar to post
Exhausted
I fall a heap.
Scattered fragments
Stand to build the vigour
Of knowing
Harshness of seeking
Clouds and hailstorms
Worries occupied rain
Tall claims of the day
Still an alibi

Moving actually is not about it
Beneath the crust
Of darkened preoccupations
Countless others ponder
Storming the way.

Bleak glimmer of satiation
You still are
Mirrored pain or pleasure

Of Partial illumination
Let go let go let go
HOLD IT
Go on

On the Eve of 1st September

Today is
The final day
Of being—last year like
The only time
I summon the monsoons
The very last time of being the self
I was not made to be
Tomorrow I may not be my former self
I would shed my skin
I will play the thought
I will put to an end—everything—forging relationship
I'd rather to start devising things not related
Thus I will burn
An effigy on time's pyre
Lit by me For me

Today is
The last time
I am passionate about 'things'
Henceforth
The objects too will be objectified
The dimensions may not change
Today is
The time I look upon as object
What you once (mis)construed
Love

D. Surya.

In the Days of Cages

Nothing seemed true; I felt surrounded by cardboard scenery which could quickly be removed

—SARTRE

When life was sitting dove like
Nestling on the wings of imagination
We ran riotous
Street to street
Screaming our hearts out.
Boisterous—our company
We were consuls'—two bodies conspiring
Amidst jargon of 'is to be morals'
Cardboard boxes, broken glasses
And Plastic talks:
Wasn't that the bottle of rum?

Inebriated—we would love still
Rummy monologues
Rummy love making
Rummy rummaging
Emptying palms
Over ill construed
Togetherness

Each day conceived
In our arms
These fanciful flights
And we would leave
Our stomachs behind
The magic of places:
Our peal reverberating
Fresh littered noon.
How we'd force fears
And live like

The last thing to do.

Every act final—so to say
Turmeric hands sweated
The wind shattered trees

Shook the muteness of space
And time commando like
Changed hands
Remained still
In the days of cages.

To Let Remain

You look at me—that tired benevolent gaze
The voices from your aching contours
Extend to my placid palms
I could crush your fragility in my embrace
Drink this moment to the last drop
And leave you to conspire
With my somnambulant diffidence
Yet this occasional tutoring helps
Every time I let go off

To let remain

Deconstruction

It takes the maturity of
An experience to perceive
That little bit of reality
Which is there and still not there
To learn real from unreal
And unlearn the learnt

(Derrida are you listening?)

On the Sight of a Surreal Painting

The stage is set

This seems the *magnum opus*
Mozart playing his requiem
As the wave lifts
The watering eyes
The horizons move
Fishes walk on the sand
The river ends mermaid finned
How the bedded desire
Lie in denture form
Inside the corked container
Within this world

A world gone berserk
Still a world

Untitled I

Live your questions now and perhaps even without knowing it,
you will live along some distant day into your answers
—RAINER MARIA RILKE

Look I flag our union
Who salutes the pards
But us
Who know of our knowing

When evening falls
Nations mourn the loss
Of heroes
But tell me
Do we have much to lose?
On the ambit of
Causation and effect.
Invigorating losses of physical pains and pleasures

Though I admit
Outgrowing losses, dispirited courage
Glorified silence
But failed to give away
Preciously guarded secrets
Between the thighs
We still look for answers
Of unanswerable
And muttered slogans steal
The music of words

Thanksgiving

Yet another year
No I am not anticipating
Losses/recovery
It's only a journey this time
From Dali to Derrida
And from Ibsen to Sartre again
Of facing

No fanciful worlds conjured
And no pinning countless hopes
Of their existence

Wonder whom to thank today
For these lovely lonesome hours
No false hopes,
No lies
No promises
No make belief affections
No lusty caresses
No forced smiles
No hard endearments
No last minute kisses—as afterthoughts

Full
Satiated today
I begin
Without these aids
And still know
I will be

Doing/not doing
With/without someone
Appears jargon
Construed recklessly

Though this year's not different
No 'cardamom tea' effect:
Yet will affect alone

No slapstick humours
No rip-roaring laughters
No pressurized talks
No comic smiles
No toady appeasements
No sexual satisfactions
No self-gratifications
No dressings over-dressing
No pointless arguments
No last minute makeup patches
No food counters waitings
No time killing buyings
No window cravings
No anxious overeatings

I thank this year
I thank this part of me

If I Could Be That Which I Am Not

All strife's continue communal feud like
Its the botheration of getting oneself explained
The task of redefining your culture, politics, religion
The journey of why you acquired a skin
Different than the rest.

Necessity of purchasing a pair of glasses
Its not that we often forget our eyes
In a group we construe like us
It's the danger of losing sight
In a crowd that's trained to
Ultimately drop eyes.

The desire of appropriation litters
The heavy baggage of guilt
The last drop of communion
Savours the taste of fellowship
On the fringes of time
You become them
(You are made so)

If born a certain way is where it all begins
Let the world raise a toast
And celebrate
As for me
I am done with celebration.

On Your Birthday

On your birthday today
I'll remember you and wish you
As long as you wish me—to remember you
To wish you 'Happy Returns'.

You might be chiding yourself not to wish so
Just as I will be chiding myself for remembering
For wanting to wish you.

You will in a way test my loyalty thus
If I do not wish you, I have an altered ego;
If I do wish you, I succumb
To countless pressures within;
Both ways I am not vindicated.

I tell myself I do not wish to do either
In countless ways you will question my 'dignity'
Purportless it is to perturb you and be perturbed in return
To remind you of the passage of time
Of you growing old and foolhardy
Of me attempting to bring back old times for old time's sake.

I remember having said in good old times
'We will celebrate your special day in a very special way'
So long you remember this;
I remember it too.
You had conveniently cut me short then
You cautiously prepared for this day,
And I kept weaving plans—incautious—unprepared—for this day

From then until now
A strange wall has been built.
I can only pretend to know the other side
While being content with this side
Lest be accused of trespassing—nay disturbing
The 'Quite' of the other side
In turn this side.

My ... (whosoever now that you are)

This day holds as much significance
As I hold to you now.

Rest all is a mind game

How agonizing can this day be?

I wait for the clock to strike twelve
For the agony to be pushed
For next year.

Relationship

We are two distant clouds
That sails adrift
That never unites
Even for the rains.

Bedroom I

Painted in blue
It distills self.
The blue floral bedspread
Cudgels me with musings
And I transform into
'A blue thought in a blue shade'

Here
Plato's 'ideal' would shy away
Aristotle's 'Catharsis', seeks no vent
Nor Browning's 'optimism' dares to comment

Sinister African masks stare
From cold damp walls
Those bark like mad dogs.
Cities of Deutschland hang uncertain in clusters
Time in a sundial calculates on calendar

The *Vincent Van Gogh* here
Awaits the return of *Ganguin*

D. SURYAWANSHI

Bedroom II

Here in my room
Light has no colour
The windows are shut for want of privacy.
The room is noisy with shrieks,
None comes—but crowded still
Its closed doors
Spell as gorgons of wrath
Bleak light flickers
When all else is dark.

The room has no lock
Yet unlocks only when
Others are locked.

Nothing is included here
Yet nothing is excluded.
Spiders and dust-bosom friends
Dine in the corner table

Here curtains are hung
For curtains sake

Bedroom III

In this bedroom

It's been some time now
The roof has become the floor
The bed still creaks
With its weight

The lungs of the blue cupboard
Are choked for breath
The hungry suitcases blue
Have got innocence packed.

Natural grotesqueries too fear
Drowning or suffocation.

Yet Life lingers
For a living housed
In lifelessness

Propria Persona

I sit and gaze at myself
The mirror stares
Cracks in silence
My body a crumpled paper
Back unloads pressure to the feet

I study the contours
Intricate creases extending with time
Curious brow
Expressionless eyes
Lifeless hair
Sunken jaws
Burdened forehead
Shoulders drooping twigs
Shrivelled bosom
Mind within stomach

Gazing once was a pleasure
Now I turn my face away
From displeasure.

Deal

We used to wonder where war lived,
what it was that made it so vile.
And now we know where it lives,
that it is inside ourselves.

—Camus

We struck a deal
Negotiated on altruistic planes
We seemed good partners—so said others
Our business got a run
'Demand and marketing' you excelled
My area remained 'supply and provision'.

'Shared profit and loss' was our motto
Your ethics later confirmed, 'Self profits only'.

You jumped the fray—the mad rat race of peers
Contemplated 'dividends & interests'.
Even set to task, the poor labour force
'Sick and slogging'—to build your economy
From a 'loose infrastructure'.

When confronted, you only said
'More work and less pay make "jack" a good boy'
You reminded me I knew nothing of 'trade',
Nothing of how to 'market'
'Finished goods' with 'polished labels'
You accused me of being 'socialist' for 'socialism'.

My 'investments' exceeded yours
For I meant to make it work
You signed the quietus of our DEAL
'Romance' and 'realism' cannot be one

I had food for thought
'Business needs to be in the blood'.

To You With Love

Love's torments sought a place of rest
Where all might drear and lonely be;
They found ere long my desert breast,
And nestled in its vacancy

—GOETHE

As I gaze at my window
At the fiery red branch of Autumn
And when I touch the thermacol flowers
Where adorned fresh carnations
Or as I enter those mute pair of slippers
That talked so often
If I look at the wrinkled body
Of the blue bedspread
Or feel the creased face
Of the blue pillow
Everything transports me to you
As if everything that exists
Food, fragrance, music, sunsets, things, memories
Were like birds
That flew towards your nests
That waits to enclose me.

Slowly if you stop loving me
I shall stop loving you slowly
Suddenly if you forget I exist
I shall forget your existence suddenly.

If you consider foolish
The pride I exude
The dignity I carry with.
If you decide to crush me

Or knowing your defeat
If you decide to forsake me
At a juncture
Where I firmly stand
Remember
On that day—on that hour
I shall hail the sky
The earth beneath
Will move awhile
And my feet shall set off
To seek greener pastures

But
If each day
My presence seems closer to you
That we bound in togetherness
If each day
A lily smiles—to whisper
On your lips—my name

Then my love—my very own
In me all those carnations blossom again
In me nothing is replaced or forgotten.
My love thrives on yours;
And as long as it lives in you
So will it be in me.

Global Conference
(A Prelude to Durban)

We met sweltering in air-conditioned hall.
Validating on the contingent parallel
Casteism = racism.
We dabbled in areas untrammelled
Live testimonials
Resolutions-hairsplitting polemics
Intellectual debates and unproven theorems
We spoke of men-women-children
The marginalization of the lowliest low
Leaders—unity—movement—in general
We saw actors-activists
Labouring with terms and phrases-onerous
Trying hard to internalize the concept anew
Casteism = Racism.

The who's who reading tailored research papers
We met self-proclaimed messiahs
Media friendly chums—delightfully raising fists
Full-throated sloganeers and drummers
Drumming parroted beats

We saw regional talks-activities
amalgamated as national
Dravidian fire becoming the spirit of oppressed
'Black' symbolized as the Dalit colour
We noticed white collareds
With deftly apprised economics.
Europeans enumerating fundamentals of
Casteism = Racism.

Amidst speeches like chants

Propositions as therapy
Documents stood under magnifying glass
For public scrutiny.

We saw folks bidding sentimental farewells
'With best regards family and friends'
'Have a safe journey until we meet again'

Everyone dispersed amidst resolves and resolutions
We saw the great grandfather's 'grand' son
Strategically chosen
For task as mammoth as representation

But they said
What we did not strategically understand
We lacked a proper vision

So proved Durban
The cause was kept away from the people

We learnt never to help our children
In their home works.

Dalit Power

But
Shouldn't we stop blaming
Stratification of society
And blame inharmonious harmony of power?
The creator god myth reverted
Ambedkar tabulated in groups
Subgroups-species and genus?
We stand there watching
'Superpowers' devouring each pigeonhole offshoot
And leaders still in elementary schools
Memorizing $2 \times 1 = 2$; $2 \times 2 = 4$;
Enriching vocabulary P for POWER
Struggling to spell U.N.I.T.Y.
We witness the horrendous growl
Turn to cats—meandering cry
We search frantically-amidst rubbles
The stern legacy of 'Dalit power'
And the local zoos and circuses
Report now and then
Of Panthers missing.

Make-up

Sometimes

I smother my face
With churlish
Makeup patches
To make up
With the world
Around me

Agonizingly

I struggle later
To make up
With myself
And my world
Around me

Drudgery

In these lonely pensive
Dark caves of my mind
Thoughts wander asunder
In quest of light
While the broad-day
Scattered awaits time
Moments as pallbearers
Keep knocking
The thin gossamer of moods
I know tomorrow is not distant:
And yet
This another day

Untitled II

Most of the times
I feel this
I feel that
And at times
When I see
The discernible
Regular faces
Of the familiar morn:

The fresh air
Undulating me
Pulsating
Passes the pulp polarity
Of my persona
And underneath
My breath
I am stifled

I am one with them
Lifeless

One Day

One day I challenged
The sun
Stared eye to eye

The 'burning sun'
Shrivelled in my gaze.

The parched entrails
Of the sky
Begged for water.

The thunder too
Has never fulminated since.

My sun shines
No more

This sun confessed
'I'd been a bastard'

On Life (Point/Counterpoint)

Point

Deceit
Empty
Brimless
Perplexing
Baffling
Fumbling
Recycling
Back to front.
Directionless
Standing as
An insidious deal
Of endless
Rumbling hopes
Ripped
In the crying belly.
Termed
What should not be
Termed

Counterpoint

Desirable
When
Cares concerns
Fret not.
Desirable
Still
When
Cares concerns
Fret.

Untitled III

Shadows flit above me
The gray curtains pull over the dome
Moment as a damsel distressed
Certain/uncertain
Time applies quick make up patches
To beautify the whole

The Jasmine Tree I

How fresh
How green
The sapling was
When I planted
At your door
How gracious it grew
To make: some linger
Hum a ballad
And wander
The thicket.
My memory struck
A deal.
To pluck
Few flowers.
While
Your stretched palms
Demanded me
The divinity dues

Elegantly the flowers
Would Transmute
To talk of beauty's birth
How delightful
The link
When you'd not be you
But the jasmine tree

The Jasmine Tree II

The days have supported months
Like conniving comrades
While years became fleeting horses
Memories turned to shadows
Now lingering guests

My dead senses fail
To reckon
The mixed fragrance
Of the jasmine tree

Beyond loyalty
The tree
Lost its belonging
A crisis of identity

The Jasmine Tree III

The final round
Of breath came
Eyes got wary of
My creation
Pallbearers' knocked
My fond reverie
Hopes arose heavenwards
I beheld
The children playing pranks
All around

I took not long
To learn the myth
Of the forbidden tree

The shrub of my jasmine
Is actually a creeper.

Still Life (Picture)

The world is a perpetual caricature of itself;
at every moment it is the mockery and the contradiction
of what it is pretending to be

—George Santayana

Mongrels growling
Orphans pleading
Motley men howling
Justice slouching
Nightingales screeching
Compassion meddling
Tradition trumpeting
Fray old wives tales
Modernity still dazed
Rolls on heavy metal
Still life
Anarchy spells doom
Skeletons drowse
Air-conditioned compartments
Available for all
Subsidy to all
Night watchmen—sleep sound
Demand for make up men
Parlours run into business.
Sizeable discounts
'With one makeup another is free'
Living far from living
Intellectuals' browsing
Pedestals of morality basking
Equity/fraternity sunbathing
Fight for right or might

Still the same
Still life
Sunken jaws ice-lolly licking
Toothless dentures nut cracking
Gods adorn cheap bars
Girls exhaust livestock
Churches scarce
Others burnt
No confession boxes anymore
Streets are red
Denizens have turned painters
Blind man's bluff
A game favoured by all

Still life

(Artists are you painting this!)

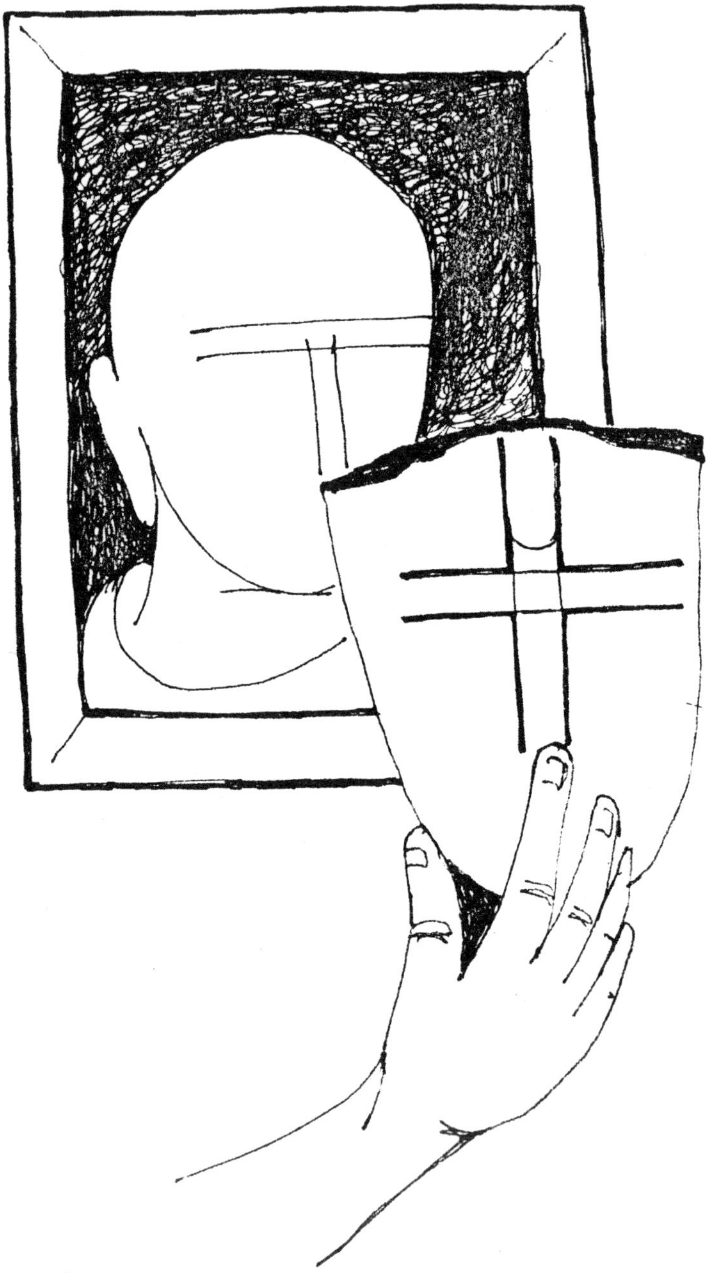

A Present

Plate of lizards
Basket of serpents
Bowl of broken dentures
Shapeless mirrors
Images of fiends
(Transfiguration)
Plate—you squat 'n' spat
Touch that turns blossoms' stone
Tongue that spews venom
Mirror that reflects past misdeeds
Images your own
(Transfiguration)

Tell me what should I
Gift you as a present?

Lines for Tomorrow

Lost in my world
Nowhere to go
From here—anymore
And hide for refuge
The bruises of past.
The fatal pride
Gives no balm.
Restless eyes
Are downward cast.
Stray mind
Stale thoughts
Give company.
Sleep like disaster
Awaits—awhile.
The monstrous dawn
Still in the womb.

Word Loss

When you call me
I lose my words.
I make vain attempts
To put them together
But I merely babble.
Purposeful intimidation
(Is that what you want?)
Is what I choose
From you.

Not that my tongue lacks
Its pristine lustre
Yet I fail to express
Or maybe to deliver

You see honey
Affectation is not my alibi
(By now you know that)
When you call me
I hear a weak thrill
Down my spine
Blood Brooklet gushes
To fill every empty pore
Then leaves a cold memory patch
From the fountain it sprung

I hear
A confrontation of heartbeats and words
Till I lose words

I am left to burn
With aching thoughts
Lost forever
Unretrieved

Advice I

My friend
She is a wind
Try holding her
She might blow you
Can you not see her thundering life?
Can you not feel her emboldened ways?
Try searching her footsteps
She will be found on untrodden ways
Judge the turbulence
She creates when she comes
Her smiles are hidden desires
Her passionate hug a craving lyre
She ruffles she knows not where
Why then link your future?
Be content when
She embalms with breezes soft
Hums you out of loneliness
Proceeds with sunshine and showers
Why do you stagnate her?
Why do you want her to stay?
Why even try holding her?
She might blow you away

Advice II

My friend
Why indulge in self-pity?
You beg alms from a heartless poor
You throw your esteem like discarded shoes
You low in servility on her demands
Why long to be loved and caressed?
When all you gain is lost
Why be good if goodness helps not?
You go out of your way to love
You get not a dime in return
Look you are the bull you plough
Better still an ass
Let go my friend
Just let go

Advice III

My friend
She might not be that heartless too
She might stir by your remonstrance
She might not be vocal as you
She howls when you speak
She's a wind
Revelation did come to you

Why deny that
Why blame her

She might be 'just' in her 'ways'
The way you are in 'your ways'
What she was is what she is
Will always be

Change your ways
If you cant change her.

Every Night

I live not in dreams but in contemplation of
a reality that is perhaps future

—Rilke

Every wishful night
I await the morn and buds to bloom
To see bright cheers amongst the groans
And see them off their glooms

Every starry night
I gather glitters in my rugged cloth
To distribute them on faces laden
With thousands of woes

Every easeful night
I die a purposeful death
To spread another revolution
To give birth to a 'sun' whose place—the hearth
And spreading fire a resolution

Every creative night
I wake up youth deep in slumbers
To impart lessons to wipe tears off
From the mournful masses

Every night I labour
To rebuild a new world.

Words

Why do words need words
To shield themselves
From the chaos
Created by words.

Why do words spell
Confusion of words
And then sit
To vindicate
By more confusion
Of words.

And its still
Only words
That we have between us

Early Morning in London

The city sleeps in silence
Houses as ghosts stand staring
A row of cars await human like in queue
Early morning walkers glance at me
Recognition a nod or a disdainful eye
In passivity I stand here at my window
While the rustle and bustle continues below
The Baker's van honk
The subway trains roar
The telecom tower—monumental stands—unhindered
A benevolent elder gazing the row of houses
The freshness of the morn emboldens the leaves
While the lamppost at Fitzroy Street blinks in azure calm
Slowly the day breaks with noises and voices
The empty Warren street come to life
The darker things are coming to light

'Good Morning' (For a Friend in SBMM)

Amidst empty chairs
Waiting for my turn to come

I see you enter
With stress laden-forehead
Distraught marks all over
Stark cold-blood solidified
Lumps of eyes-covering your face
Layers of scattered skin
Thrown all around
You walk in to greet me with a smile

'Good morning' you say
And my day begins

Standing by the Thames

Waters of Thames glittered
As brisk as memories
Torn between Bridge and the Tower.
Ships are asunder
Scattered as thoughts
On mind waters
The tidal parlance
As gospel divine

Whoever said gone is the serenity
Could never feel the masters
That stood the immortal shores
Where now
My feet firmly stand.
Ready then as now
To heed
The enraptured callings

Could never realize
The divide of experience and expression
The stirrings of life
In the inconceivable dead
As I do—the profundity
Of my feeling
As it sinks the soul

A Chant

Don't tell me someday someone
Is the one for you
So tell me now
Do I need to hang on or move apart

My eyes are weary to watch the hurt inside
My breathing has lost the rhythm divine
I know I need you and yet need you not
So tell me now
Do I need to hang on or move apart

Weathers change like men in colours
There are mountains of guilt between
One another
Don't try to be what not you are
So tell me now
Do I need to hang on or move apart

Call me not 'just a friend to share'
You know you are
Something more than friend
Why then burden the brow
With a heavy pretence
So tell me now
Do I need to hang on or move apart

Spilt persona you are not
I feel the oceans deep-feeling
Nestling in you
My trust rounds and ends to be with you
Let me repose now or never
Let me never ask you again
To tell me now
Do I need to hang on or move apart

Wish I Was Not Born At All

At times I wish
I was not born at all
To watch the spectacle
Of madness gripping humankind

Nervous fanatics—fever gripped
Unholy tongues chanting
Hare Rama Hare Krishna!
Voicing Christ as a foreigner
Ostracizing Buddha from his native land

Religious doctrines taught with religious hatred
Holy men with unholy deeds
Priestly robes blood stained
Devotees offerings better halves for placements
Abject servility for visa to dreamland
Pedestals of inhumanity
Voicing for national concerns
Governing bodies—hot beds of speculation

Envoys from distant lands
Discuss global economy
The ragged man on the street
Steals when none heeds him
We pray we no not to whom
We live we no not for what
We martyr we no not the cause
We sustain we no not how to retain
A generation with potent talent
A befuddled legacy for a stupefied race

No: this was not the fight
Of the real ones
Martyred for this land
I swear by the noose
Around Bhagat Singh's neck

At times I wish
I was not born at all

Reciprocation

Look the golden hub has faded
In the distant sky
And your honeyed words
Still wrapped around me
Have blushed me pink

Like the motion of a captured fish
My heart flutters before giving in
To your omnipresence

In This Democracy My Eyes Search

Beauty's been caught lying
And the truth rubbed raw
Here, you get your remorse
As a constitutional right
—RITA DOVE

My eyes search a free man
Whose breath is not pawned
And whose living is not an installment premium
Demanding space
Demanding mercy of laissez faire
Whose dreams are not attuned to power whims
Nor who accommodates politico creeds

My eyes search a free man
Whose aspiration is not elite dictated
In bureaucratic/plutocratic run
Codifying conventions for
'Simple living high thinking'
Whose joy is not planned for cut-throat market
Whose needs are not privatized for neo-liberalist gain

My eyes search a free man
Whose religion is not state chosen
Nor by nation with ownership right
Persuading ethics in immoral proportions
Whose death is not forecasted by community feuds
No quietus signed for non-affiliates

My eyes search a free man
Whose voice is not stifled as fanatic propagation
Of dehumanized sensitivity

For untold miseries/lies
Whose world is not an obligation
Of peremptory needs
Whose conscience is not subjugated
To passion's slavery

My eyes but search a free man
In this democracy

In Such Endless Infuriating Nights

In such endless infuriating nights
When despair—naked
Glances eye-to-eye
The dark deferred hopes
The apertures of mind
Refill—The endorsed fore vision
Of countless Musings
Uninterrupted
By slow muttering sobs
Augmented by the vanquished regret
For a visionary's vision lost

I Fear

I fear I may be gone forever
Leave no imprints
On the sands of times.
Fade in the enraptured
Chasm of the night.
Dissolve as an insignificant bubble
In the fathomless depths
Of nothingness.

Contemporary Dust

There is much dust around me
I cannot clean
Falls on my apartment
From the living room
Travels to the attic
Then moves to the study
At times falls on me
I brush off with casual effort
Wash myself now and then
To hurry for work
I find my office full of dust
How can this be?
I wonder.

I cannot deny
The winds mischief
But what potent source
Generously contributes it
In such a monastery
Green foliage covered?

The dusty dust that at once stops
The breathing breath
I cannot figure how
I try to manoeuvre
Look for the sources
I find my co-workers room
Full to the brim

Dust had a catharsis
Excess over flew to my room
They were comfortable with it

They lived with it
Year's together—seasons together
Schooled to do so.
Charity shows contributed dust cleaners
Which were cleaned away.

I got to know how this dust
Comes to stay
I take to my heels
Labour to clean the dust
I succeed to some extent
And shut my doors
To check the flow

To others I remark with a sigh
'Dust thou art to dust thou shall return.'

A Sentence

I spread my wings wide open
To embrace the sky
I welcome you
Into my world
Simple/complex/compound

Taste the unknown

I languidly desire
Your companionship
Of no returns

Illusion and Reality

As I could not reach the moon anymore
I asked it to 'please come down'
And lend it to me

I reminded how it'd come running
With delicate damsel steps
To the calling of poetry
A humble page in pages of art
Wasn't it then a symbol
Of high romance
Glorified youth
Idealized love?

It smiled to frown afar
I said
'Come'
'Let me hold you in my palm'

Resistant yet anxious
It fell to the ground
The earth made way
'Received its honoured guest'

Trees hummed a strange melody
Obstinate bees sucked harder
The honeyed oaths from flowers lips
Symphonic birds tuned in cadenza
Squall of rain whistled past
As disgruntled clouds connived
For the storms to come
To break and subside

I stood in this Louvre
A Venus d'Mello
Absorbing and absorbed
By this curious transformation
Between nature and self.

Passionate onlookers stared
In geometrical dimensions
To report with caution
A strange phenomenon

One day I asked the moon
To 'please come down'

Thought Process

Hellish darkness pervades
Mental aberrations in swing
Out of circular wriggling-swirling
A lambasting paranoia
Etching millions black blue
Curves in continuum
Uncanny clamour of some obstinate
Buzzing bee
Sonorous with each curvature
Cosmic branching to ad infinitum
A heavy sumptuous
Incognito bog
Swelling in mounds
As potent volcanic energy
A meteor shoots out of the ensemble
Of matter:
The cycle is complete.

Lines Composed in My Room at Uppsala, Sweden

I sit here in complete harmony
The world out there speaks monotony
Rigorous battles fought long ago
Regular slogans for tomorrow
Expressing resentment for undone sorrows

While I sit here in complete harmony
Lucky to hold an alien chamber
Battles lost baffle me not
Regularity now becomes trifle
Resentment any seems illegible

As I am in complete harmony here.

On the Sight of a Chameleon

Every second day I glance a chameleon
Easy on the bark of my jasmine plant
Rattling up rattling down
Changing colours at will
Wobbling an innocent prey
Haply unaware
Of fiend complacent

In lieu of shame
Pretends to camouflage
Seems to be
A knight with shinning armour to me
Witless and crafty
A wizard to foresee

After the fill remains still
Seems the one who manages
To save his skin
Yet I fail to understand
Why I enjoy such grotesqueries nigh

With the changing pastels
Of my vicinity
A desire secret within me peeps
Could I ever be the one
Easy on the bark
Of my jasmine plant?

But then I cannot ignore
The many at large

Someone ought to also be
An innocent prey.

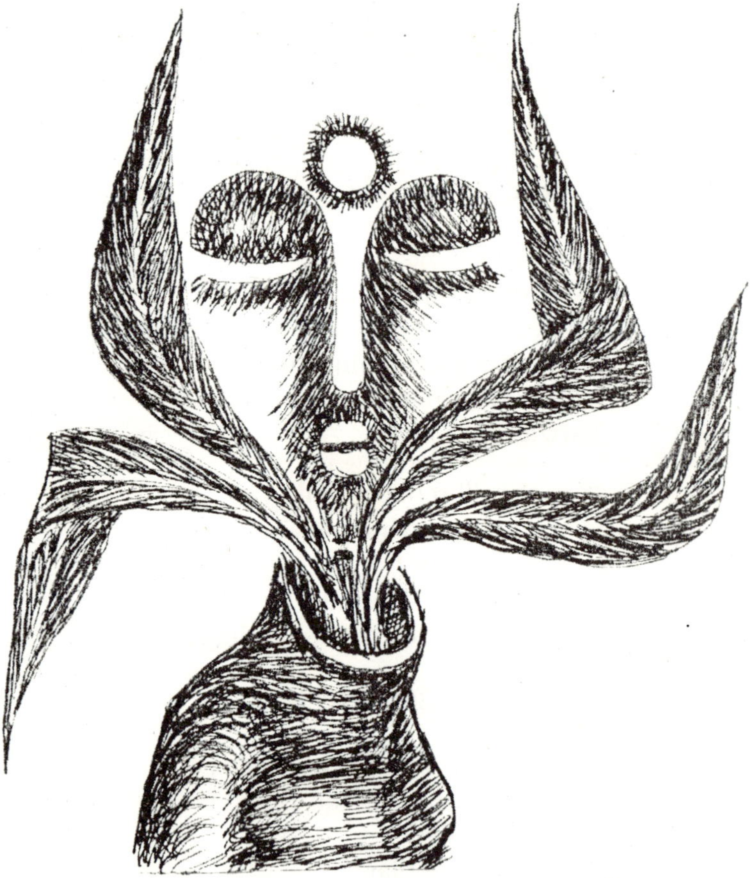

Habituate

In the deserts I roam
Poisoned loaf I eat
Wine I drink
I hear countless groans
Faces confront—marked
With infernal smiles
Deliberate mocks

In these deceptive appearances
I am misfit pronounced for time

I appease myself
Think of woes I know
Yet breed perturbed mind
Feed still—the soul with
Poisoned loaf I eat
Wine I drink

In the deserts I roam
I habituate myself
For time.

In This Deep Dark Maze

In this deep dark maze
Holding to a ray of light
By my pillow
I submit myself
To the power of drowsiness

Hopes, desires, aspirations
That gets enslaved
To the dark night
Compel men only to be sleep drunk

Over digressive tidal waves
On the vessel of perpetual orthodoxy
Of a long standing
Seems my journey

Cutting across
The dreary silence
My voice tries to communicate
To me...

And on such an endless day
Is carved a seal
To live
As a man.

D. Suryawanshi

Grace (For a Tamasha Artist)

Sky saddened
Starlets silent
Graveyard slumbers
With dead moralists

Somewhere far-off
The night has come of age
Between the sheets of cadenced music
The clinking of anklets

Inebriated footprints hint
She—alone
They—Many

On her painted face are carved
Pursuits and records
History of every night

Unruffled gaze
Disinterested movements
Lost somewhere far-off is
The grace of her living

I Float on the Surfaces of these Immeasurable Silences

I float on the surfaces of these immeasurable silences
A voice amidst voiceless-ness
Stifled by regularization of private needs
Penalized for being what I should not be
And not being what I ought to be
I reach out each to each
For those godforsaken vows of bliss and togetherness
Left high and dry amidst those ceaseless chanting of
  insufficiencies
Choked with logical demands
I am left high and dry
To be comfortable in discomforts
I bear all the pangs alone
I bear all the brunt alone

Dhammagiri I

The glistening golden dome
In sanguine majesty
Resplendent amidst
The overshadowing green hills
The tinklings from the spire
Reverberating the freshest morn ever born
The silent narrow lanes
The distanced bylanes
Crisscrossing the dandelions and wild pansies
The row houses like monks
In quite meditation bowing
In reverence to the prayer hall
The tranced inmates jostle past
In expressionless countenance
The birds in unison chirp
'Bhavtu sabba mangalam'
Perched on the flora
On the loftiest branches
The butterflies whisper
'Anichya Anichya'

No choristers or banisters here
To rapture glories
Of the ensuing day
Yet never before was the dawn
So delightfully lyrical
The pygmy sun seems shamed
By the mighty presence of the dome
Vainly now hid behind the hills
To indulge in its favourite pastime

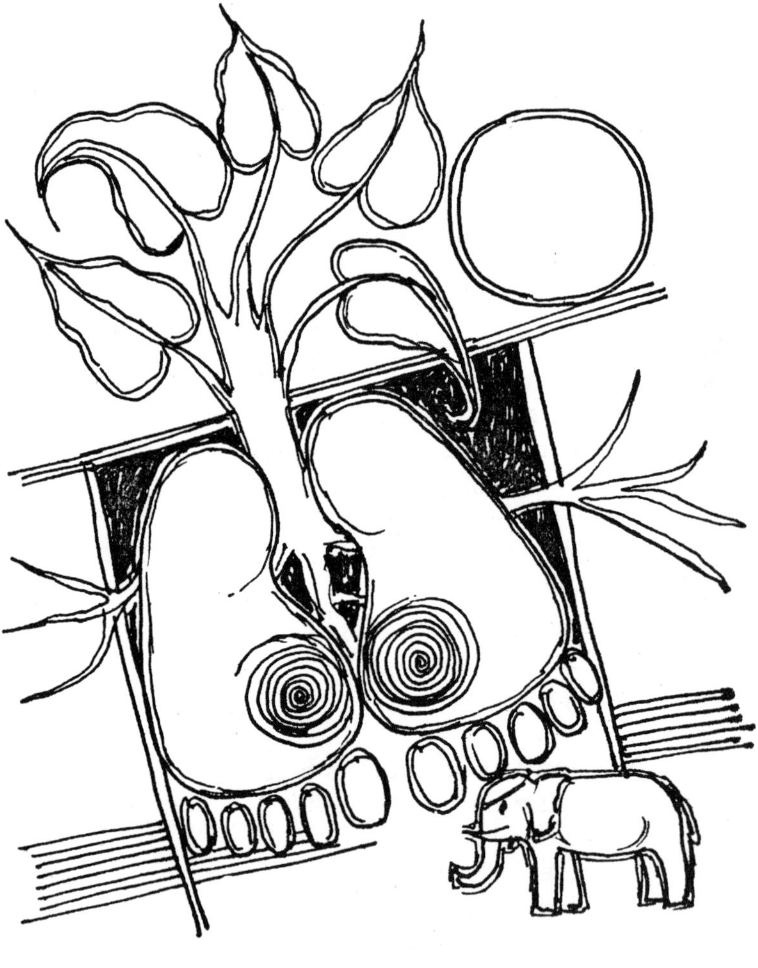

Dhammagiri II

Here at Dhammagiri
The blessed day closes
Leaving some mystery unfolded
The fireflies then rejoice
Ready to flaunt their talent
To the passing night
When gnats hum a melancholy strain
The moon too intrudes
The solitary cottages
Arrayed as sentinels
The winds eavesdrop
The discourse of mind and senses

Whilst its pages conspire
To create rhythm like chant
Orchestrated by rustling leaves
Peace descends gradually
Thickens amid the grooves.
'Buddham sarnam gachyami'

Dhammagiri III

Here at Dhammagiri
You hear not of noble miracles
Of clash of powers,
Of violent battles
Or of concocted myths
Nor does one surmise
Fables of sectarianism,
Or of deprivation of rights.
The path to *Nirvana*
Slowly get subtler
As sensations begin
To speak to the mind
The pragmatism of sense experience
Banish perplexities, hindrances
Routine beliefs and doubts
Now Rationale stands face to face
All other dogmas preached
By 'blind mouths' of outside world
Are left mutilated forever
Every uplifted being
Grapples with a renewed awakening
'I too can become the Buddha'
A world within a world

Blessed is the township
Doubly blessed the state
Thrice blessed the nation
The host to the abode

Secure and Untouched
Every object here throbs
By the wonder of *dhamma*
'Atta Deep Bhava'

Choice

As I drive the regular
West High Court drive way
The vacant narrow streets
Grace my presence
I cross the myriad ways
Of the stifled lanes
Breathing the cosmopolitan air
I perceive a grim battle
Surging inside

I see a row of breathless mummies
Crowding the streets—obstructing
I tell myself
'I should have taken another way'
Or 'then was this the only way'
Or 'a way'

Now! Now! Need to make peace
Call for truce
Forget the way—I came and go.

Once again I glance
The naked west high court roads
Hail to myself
How horridly hollow are both!

The Sacred Beast of Longing

The sacred beast of longing
Brings me so far to your land
So arid, dry and unblessed
Fruitless yearnings turn to accursed aspersions

Are your words still very much yours
Or broken arrows disarrayed
Aimed only for the stars that build
Desires and greater longings

How foolish of me to imagine
Transmutation of artificial flowers for real
'Imagined glories have bitterness of greater consequence
Than unimagined pleasures'
Should I then stop all—once for all

Else tell me
How do I quench
This sacred beast of longing.

In Response to What a Known Poet Said to an Unknown

'You have a long way ahead'
'Grow up'
'Your poetry needs to grow up'

And I say
How do I grow up?
How does my poetry grow up?
I have a long way ahead
What about the long one left behind?

'Poetry is not anybody's business'
'To write poetry one needs to be poetic'

(Now whatever that means)
Rhyme-rhythm-figures-imagery-intact.

'Bring images of unknown worlds'
'Make it interesting'

But how to ignore the known world
And get poetic in un-poetic times.

Certainly poetry is not my forte then
I agree with the ageing poet
Who had last said this to me
So next time I write
I must get my words
Approved to see
If they are placed the way he wants
So as to make my poetry appealing to his taste buds
After all doesn't all poetry require

To be 'chewed and digested?' *(Sorry Mr. Francis Bacon)*
Like the way many poets are swallowed these days
Doesn't it require to be advertised in biased magazines?
Or doesn't it require being subject to an audience poll?
Only then can it come in a book form.
And the person gets *christened* as poet

Well I achieved nothing of this
Not in fame nor in words
My words flow un-chiselled
Un-frilled-un-clad
And still I am reminded
I need to grow up
That I have a long way ahead
That poetry is a business just for few
To bring images of unknown worlds
To make it interesting
How prosaic that sounds
Harsh but true?

Long Live the Queen

Branded cockerel with diasporic experiences
Nostalgia and riotous imaginations
Is what makes one a better poet than the other
This added with a heap of poetic nothings
And several collections to boast of.
Here a manufacturer can become a poet.
Not a writer

What establishes one de-establishes the other
So has it not happened with poets and poetry?
The ringleader leads the taming process
He commands the roast and the barbeque.

And with a lump throat-stuck

The poor bidden guest is left to remark
'It was a delightful meal'

And for me

'Sorry sir
My creative prowess has been stifled
By centuries of labour
Rubbing my back on your backyards
My palms have chaffed
Praying to unknown gods
When you read and interpreted
I waited outdoors for leftovers
When you indulged in poetic leisure
I was making both ends meet
So, sir if I write poetry
This is my take
I will present images only of the world known
To you and to me.

One Evening

To lessen
The languor
Of its exhausted body
The sun descends
In the ocean

The night coats its cheeks
With scarlet of the sundown

In the world of dreams
The crippled shores of the 'being'
Are touched by
The mesmerized waves
The iced tears
Find their way

One evening
Wrapped in the limitless storm
Stands against me
Emblazoned
For a bright morrow.

When I Announced Today

When I announced today
I was to go against the waves.
Surprisingly, the waves kept mum

Once so full 'of sound and fury'
Their deafening roars mellowed
And dashed aimlessly
On these weather beaten
Ancient walls of Academia

Once a Queen in Royal robes
So full of regalia and royalty
Today patched in leper's cloth
She is out begging for alms

The walls are gone brittle
Ready to crumble any moment
Some portion has given way already
The helpless birds safely perched on them
Have dived hopelessly for lifejackets.
Frantically, searching for the remnants
Nothing left to cling to anymore.

They have hired a pigeon for some lakhs
To Negotiate Business with
Dryden, Pope, Johnson, Addison
Keats, Wordsworth, Coleridge, Shelley, Byron,
Eliot, Yeats, Auden, Hopkins,
Shakespeare, Shaw, Webster, Milton.
To critique
Plato, Aristotle, Sophocles, Barthes, Derrida, Fish,
Habermas, Bodkin, Iser, Lukacs, Eagleton,

Jacobson, Lyotard, Hall, Bhabha, Fanon
To communicate English to
Moore, De Beauvoir, Wollstonecraft,
Woolf, Showalter, Rich, Spivak, Millett,
Mitchell, Morrison, Giovanni, Walker, Angelou,
Roy, Desai

They have also transported a parrot
To predict their future in tarot cards.
And decide the doomsday of the sprawling structure.
Earlier the better.
To avoid a virulent boil on the ass
Moonstone is recommended
To stop the virus of 'scratching each others back'
A cat's eye is the best bet.

They have bought a maina* from the cheapstreet
To entertain them
She sings a filmy tune now and then
And keeps her customers thoroughly satisfied.

They have sent ravens to croak around
Being ill-fed they drop their mouthing
For better morsels offered.

When I announced today
I was to go against the waves.
Surprisingly, the waves kept mum

I shouted back at the immensity
With all my strength
I shall not live to bend neither bend to live.

I have lifted a wave and wafted it on the clouds
Now I will decide the fall
Henceforth I will decide the end

*Maina: a songbird.

Lines Written Upon Kovalam Beach

As the lovelorn waves kiss and depart
The sand beneath my feet
Tickles and sifts and melts
The magnitude of the pull is large
As I hear the distant seas roaring
To the unknown far-off lands
The white foam surfs ahead
And then reluctantly recedes
It has me wooed already
I walk dazed
Turn to look back at my footprints
To feel only a vision I left of them
A mighty exalted wave comes to wash them away
And others and still others too.
I shoo a crab back into the hole
Jubilant at this one
A sailor on an un-balanced skiff
Struggles with his fast limbs
Not once giving way.
A wooden shaft like boat
Jostles unmindful of the fierce sea
That tosses it with might
And far in the horizons stand
Ships as sentries guarding the deep dark

A couple now hand in hand chirping pass by
A fun filled day at sea with togetherness
Is all that matters to them.
While a silent somebody gazes at the sinking sun
The darkness collects around my patch of sky
I wait for the sun to die.

Acknowledgements

My parents for orchestrating this significant initiation into the poetic province and for loving me large enough to let go.

Shubroto, Rina, Akhil, my soulmates and pals for loving daily and fighting daily.

Nikhil for a living memory of his unforgettable presence around me each day.

Dr. Sutinder Singh Noor, writer, critic and a dear friend for the structural solidity of an infallibly and incredibly honest critique.

Namdev Dhasal, my earliest reader, critic and closest admirer, for giving me the strength to carry on. For defying linguistic barriers to lend voice to my creation.

Dilip Suryawanshi for ceremoniously saying it with images where words pause.

My publishers for making the book see the daylight.

Thank you.